# Granny Go

## Gifts

Granny Garcia was moving
to a smaller house.
Her family came to help.
Granny had too many
things, so they put some of
them in her front garden.

Granny made a big sign.
It said: *Please, help yourself
to Granny Garcia's gifts.*

Please, help yourself to Granny Garcia's gifts.

5

Later that day, Molly from next door passed Granny Garcia's front garden.
She saw a lampshade.
It was old and dusty.

"I can use this,"
she said to herself.

Please,
help yourself
to Granny
Garcia's gifts.

Molly took the lampshade home. She cleaned off the dust. She painted it blue. Then she got some shells that she had found on the beach and glued them onto the lampshade.

8

In the afternoon,
Mr. Ryan from along
the street walked his dog
past Granny Garcia's house.
He saw some old bits
of wood.

"I could make something with these," he said to himself.

Mr. Ryan took the pieces of wood home to his shed. He made them into photo frames. He decorated them with flowers and leaves.

13

That evening, Mrs. Watson from the end of the street was walking home from work. She noticed a tin tub in Granny Garcia's front garden.

"I have been looking
for something like this,"
Mrs. Watson said to herself.
"This will look good
in my garden."

Mrs. Watson took
the tub home and gave
it a wash and a scrub.
She put holes in the
bottom and painted it
green. Then she planted
some flowers in it.

16

The children who lived next
to Mrs. Watson's house
went past Granny Garcia's
garden. Maria read the sign
to Sam and Sara.

"Look, there are wheels,
ropes, and a wooden box,"
said Sam.

"Let's make a cart!"
the children all cried.

The children put
the wheels and ropes
inside the wooden box.
The three of them
carried the box home.

It took them two days
to put the things together
and make a cart.

A week later, Granny Garcia was ready to move. All her friends threw a surprise party for her.

"Good luck!" they shouted. Then they gave her gifts for her new home.

"Thank you," said Granny Garcia. "These will remind me of you."

23

"Thank *you*, Granny Garcia," said everyone. "All our things will remind us of *you*!"